AMPLE ANIMALS

WRITTEN by GEMMA PETERS

ILLUSTRATED by ANDY STARK

Gemma Peters is currently teaching English to primary school children in the U.K., with a particular passion for creative writing. Her idea in creating the text was to incorporate the sing-song rhythm of Shakespeare's iambic pentameter with alliteration. To introduce these two important literary motifs to young children she used the theme of animals; each with a corresponding letter of the alphabet. To further attract the young audience, she chose the artist Andy Starck to depict each animal scene with strong vivid illustrations in bright colourful settings.

Andy Starck is an artist based in Taiwan, where he lectures at Southern Taiwan University in subjects ranging from Philosophy, History to Creative Writing.
A graduate from St. Martin's School of Art, having spent half of his life in Asia mostly in Taiwan he has become ever more influenced by the East. Now immersed in Chinese Calligraphy he also has great interest in the aboriginal tribal art and culture of Taiwan.

傑瑪‧彼得斯特別喜歡創作，目前任教於聯合王國的小學。她的創作理念結合傳統頭韻與莎翁時期盛行的抑揚格五音步。為了讓小朋友熟悉這兩種寫作技巧，她運用各種動物的開頭字母，以頭韻詩與抑揚格五音步，融入小朋友喜愛的動物主題。此外，傑瑪與旅居台灣多年的英籍藝術家，安迪‧史塔克合作，以鮮明的色彩插畫敘述每一則動物故事。

安迪老師任教於南臺科技大學應用英語系。早年畢業於英國聖馬丁藝術學院，目前於南臺教授哲學與創作史等課程。由於旅台多年，其藝術觀深受東方思想薰陶。目前除了醉心於書法創作外，也多所涉獵台灣原住民藝術與文化。

Have you heard of Shakespeare? Can you name anything he wrote? Maybe you know Romeo and Juliet, Hamlet or King Lear. These were all plays performed at the theatre. But Shakespeare had a special way of writing, it was called iambic pentameter. This is a musical rhythm that stresses the second syllable, di-dum, di-dum, di-dum, di-dum, di-dum. Every sentence in this book uses this rhythm. If you look carefully you may also notice the first letter of each word in a sentence is the same. This is called alliteration, another literary technique.

This is a children's book but some of the vocabulary is not so easy, so adults reading this book can also improve their language skills. Every letter of the alphabet has a picture of an animal doing something. Enjoy the colourful illustrations, each one was hand painted by the artist Andy Starck.

你們認識莎士比亞嗎？知道他寫過什麼作品嗎？或許你們聽過《羅密歐與茱麗葉》、《哈姆雷特》或《李爾王》，這些都是耳熟能響的舞台劇，但你們知道這些劇本是已抑揚格五音步寫成的嗎？這種詩歌的節奏重音落在第二音節，呈現輕重、輕重、輕重、輕重、輕重等十音節的韻律。這本書每一句都是依此韻律寫成，而且各位如果細心閱讀，會發現句中每一個字第一個字母相同，這就是頭韻。

雖然這是一本童書，但是有些字彙不見得淺顯易懂，因此成年讀者閱讀也可增加字彙量喔。此外，每一字母有其代表動物，並佐以安迪老師親筆創作生動有趣的插畫。

石耀西簡介
(南臺科技大學應用英語系助理教授/台南科學園區英語顧問)

AuthorHouse™ UK
1663 Liberty Drive
Bloomington, IN 47403 USA
www.authorhouse.co.uk
Phone: 0800.197.4150

Published by AuthorHouse 07/16/2019

ISBN: 978-1-5462-9272-2 (sc)
978-1-5462-9271-5 (e)

Library of Congress Control Number: Pending

Print information available on the last page.

Any people depicted in stock imagery provided by Getty Images are models,
and such images are being used for illustrative purposes only.
Certain stock imagery © Getty Images.

This book is printed on acid-free paper.

Because of the dynamic nature of the Internet, any web addresses or links contained in this book may have changed
since publication and may no longer be valid. The views expressed in this work are solely those of the author and do
not necessarily reflect the views of the publisher, and the publisher hereby disclaims any responsibility for them.

authorHOUSE®

One sunny summer's day,
the Ample Animals go on their
annual picnic.

Arthur Armadillo
adores acorns

Betty Bear brings
beautiful bananas

Caroline Cat
consumes copious cod

David Dog devours
delicious dates

Ed Elephant eats
everyone else's!

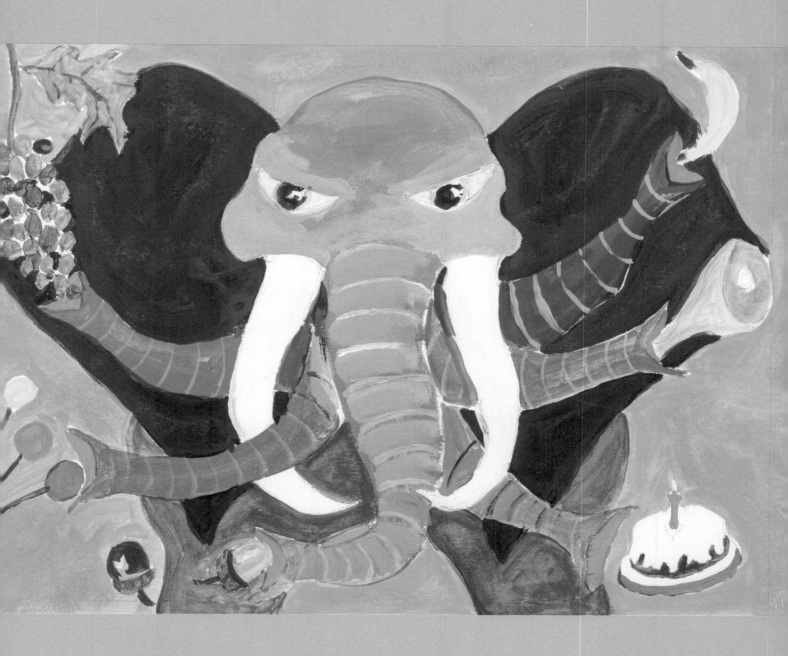

Freda Fish favours
flavourful flake food

Gary Giraffe guzzles grapes greedily

Hannah Hyena
has heavenly ham

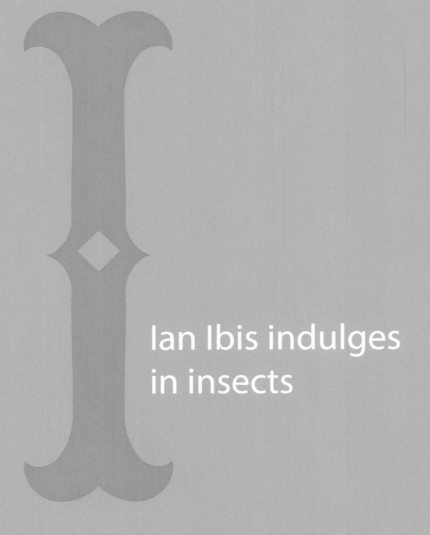

Ian Ibis indulges
in insects

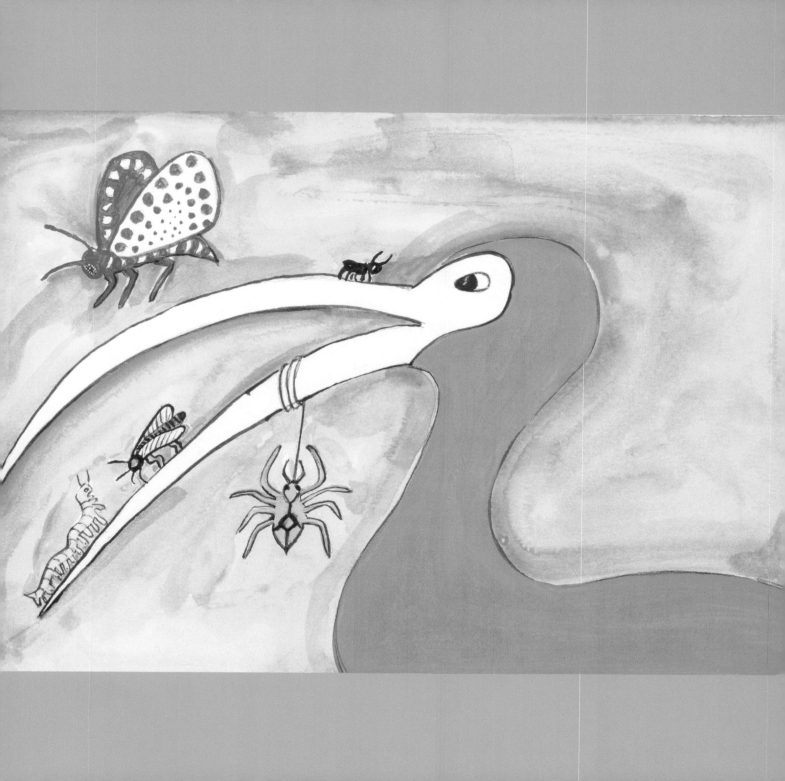

Jack Jaguar jams
in juicy jelly

Kathy Kangaroo
keenly kicks kippers

Lucinda Lama
licks lovely lollies

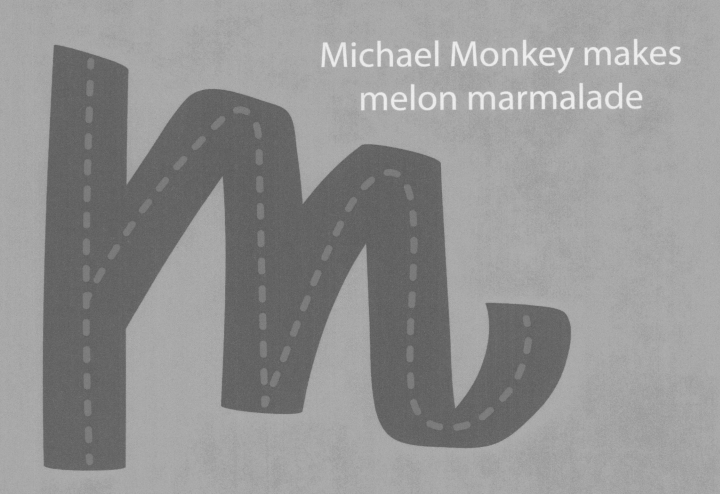

Michael Monkey makes
melon marmalade

Nina Nightingale
nibbles noodles

Oliver Ostrich
opens orange oats

Patricia Panda
prefers perfect peas

Quinton Quail
quietly quivers quiche

Rachel Rabbit
really rates rich, red rice

Sid Snake sneakily
sizzles sausages

Tina Tiger
takes tea to the tortoise

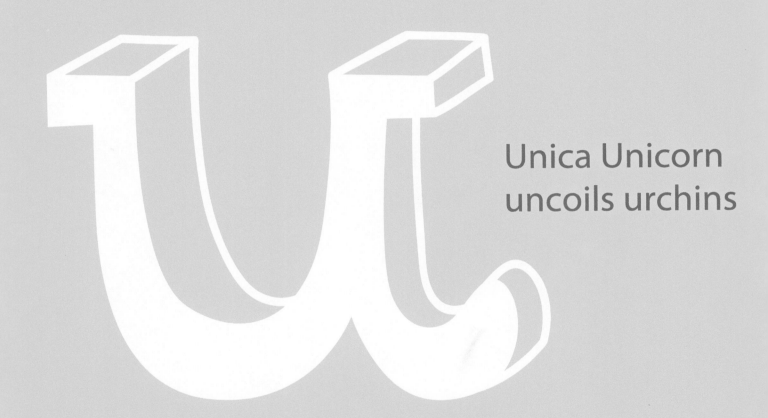

Unica Unicorn
uncoils urchins

Vic Vixen views
various vegetables

Winston Wolf
wants white waffles with walnuts

Xena's xylophone
xeroxes Xouba

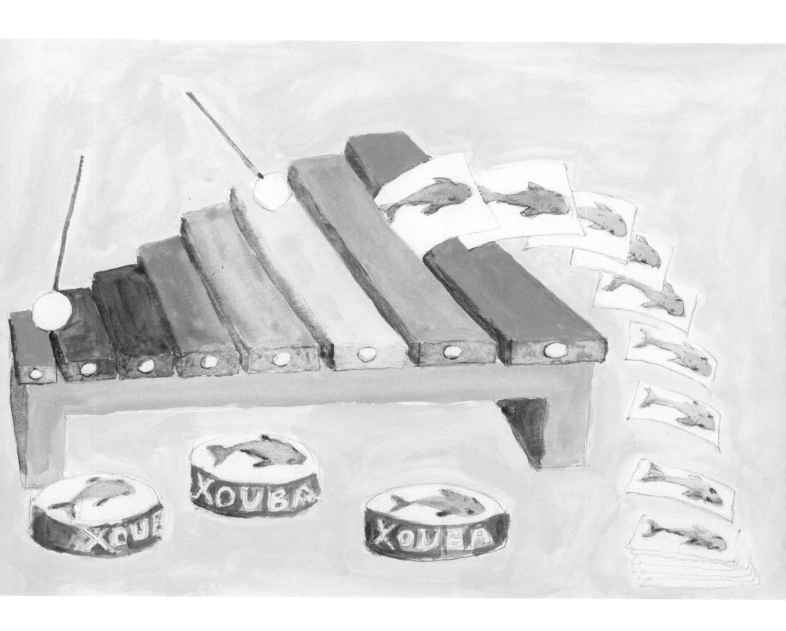

Yaden Yak yields
yesterday's yogurt

Zoe Zebra zigzagged zucchini zest

Name the tortoise who Tina takes tea to.
Remember that this must begin with the letter T.